Joni Hudson-Reynolds

# *Take Your* Dream *out of* Layaway

WESTBOW
PRESS®
A DIVISION OF THOMAS NELSON
& ZONDERVAN

This book is a work of non-fiction. Unless otherwise noted, the author and the publisher make no explicit guarantees as to the accuracy of the information contained in this book and in some cases, names of people and places have been altered to protect their privacy. WestBow Press books may be ordered through booksellers or by contacting:

Scripture taken from the Holy Bible, NEW INTERNATIONAL VERSION®. Copyright © 1973, 1978, 1984, 2011 by Biblica, Inc. All rights reserved worldwide. Used by permission. NEW INTERNATIONAL VERSION® and NIV® are registered trademarks of Biblica, Inc. Use of either trademark for the offering of goods or services requires the prior written consent of Biblica US, Inc.

Two Chapter 4 Scripture quotations taken from the 21st Century King James Version®, copyright © 1994. Used by permission of Deuel Enterprises, Inc., Gary, SD 57237. All rights reserved.

WestBow Press
A Division of Thomas Nelson & Zondervan
1663 Liberty Drive
Bloomington, IN 47403
www.westbowpress.com
1 (866) 928-1240

Because of the dynamic nature of the Internet, any web addresses or links contained in this book may have changed since publication and may no longer be valid. The views expressed in this work are solely those of the author and do not necessarily reflect the views of the publisher, and the publisher hereby disclaims any responsibility for them.

Any people depicted in stock imagery provided by Thinkstock are models, and such images are being used for illustrative purposes only. Certain stock imagery © Thinkstock.

ISBN: 978-1-4908-9834-6 (sc)
ISBN: 978-1-4908-9835-3 (e)

Library of Congress Control Number: 2015911646

Print information available on the last page.

WestBow Press rev. date: 07/30/2015

# DEDICATION

*This book would not be possible without the love of my life, my husband Alex. He has been my rock and my chief cheerleader. I also want to acknowledge my two wonderful children, Alex and Alicia. I taught them to Dream Big, and they have taught me to keep Dreaming Big. They inspire me every day.*

*To my late parents, Charles and Mozella Hudson, I thank them for working hard and teaching me that if I worked hard, I could do anything. I also cannot forget my uncle, William Fitzgerald who has been a second father to me, and my favorite and only sister, Vicki Hudson, who is a living example of a miracle-working God. I am blessed to have her in my life.*

*To my many friends, I thank you all for listening to me talk, and talk, and talk about this book.*

*Last, but certainly not least I thank God for this moment and for this dream.*

*Let's start taking the dream out of layaway.*

# FORWARD

*Take the first step today. Your dream will not only bless you, but it will bless others through you.*

This book is designed for people who have a dream, but they have simply allowed the dream to be dormant for too long. It's for people who yearn for more in life, but simply don't know how to get their dream out of layaway. Maybe you have looked at the dream and made some baby steps, but you stopped.

You wonder how to transition from the dream that is only real in your head to making that dream really happen. Perhaps you think now you have waited too long or you are too old. I've got one question for you, are you dead? If you are reading this I already know the answer. You are not, but you know this is your time and you have got to take action. Start moving...Today. Your dreams are so important don't give them up helping others fulfill *their destiny*.

# CONTENTS

# CONTENTS

*For I know the plans I have for you, declares the Lord, plans to prosper you, plans to give you hope and a future.* -Jeremiah 29:11

# INTRODUCTION

When I grew up my parents often put things in layaway. I am talking old school layaway. What they would do is pick out the items at the store that they wanted and they would put a down payment on the items. They had a certain amount of days that the store would hold the items for them, and during that time period they would make payments on the items. If they failed to make the payments in the agreed amount of time the store would return the items to the sales floor and my parents would forfeit their payments. The magical thing about layaway is it gave you the ability to brag to your friends about the items you had on layaway. You would hear people saying "I have a sharp, black leather coat on layaway."

## LAYAWAY TAKEAWAY:

**Layaway gave you the ability to live your dream without truly possessing it.**

Many of us have put our dreams on layaway. For some reason we have put the dream away and established valid reasons why we simply cannot get it out. We will still talk about the dream, but once we stop talking the dream quietly goes back into the layaway. We have what we believe are valid reasons not to pursue the dream. Most of them are familiar: we're married, we've got children, our jobs are too demanding or we simply don't have time. We still talk about the dream, but we say I will do this, but only after I do that and this gives us a false sense of ownership. We never make the payment and then we ultimately forfeit our dream. But this is the time to finally take your dream out of the layaway and that is what we are going to do.

**Before you start reading the book take a little time and fill out the Dream Worksheet.**

# DREAM WORKSHEET

1. What is my dream?

2. Why do I want to accomplish it?

3. Will it help me?

4. Will it help others?

5. What am I willing to do to make it happen?

6. What am I willing to sacrifice?

7. How does the thought of your dream make you feel?

8. How will I feel if I don't take my dream out of layaway?

9. Do I really believe that God gave me this dream?

10. What is stopping me?

# CHAPTER 1

# Finding The Dream Again

As I write this book I am in a new place in life. I had to make a change. Most of us resist change because change can be challenging, but sometimes change is forced upon us. We are not given the luxury of deciding if we want to make a change – someone else makes that decision for us. I was forcibly ejected from my comfort zone.

A few years ago I was the media director for a non-profit. It was a job I felt comfortable doing and I felt I was really helping people, but there was something missing. If you are comfortable you often simply want things to stay the same, even if you don't feel that you are truly operating in your "sweet spot." I never thought of quitting, but I went on a vacation and the day I got back my boss said he wanted to meet with me. I thought he wanted to simply give me a new assignment, but to my surprise, he let me go. Yes he let me go. The company was downsizing and my job was regarded as nice but not necessary. So I spent the first few months being sad, and the next few months being mad, and then I finally accepted it. By then, the economy had tanked and jobs were scarce, but somehow I still managed to finally see the blessing in the storm.

## LAYAWAY TAKEAWAY:

**Too often we seek the blessing in a safe space, and that might have been the place to be for a time, but we have to recognize when we no longer fit in that space.**

Over the past six years I have done a variety of jobs, including: summer camp director, communication consultant, public relations specialist for a charter school, freelance writer, blogger and school aftercare worker. What I have learned along the way? Each of these experiences has put me in the position to write this book. My comfort zone is now a distant memory, but in order to grow sometimes you have got to let go.

The comfort zone does not encourage growth. Sometimes the challenge and the blessing are in the uncertain. As Martin Luther King said, "Faith is taking the first step even when you can't see the whole staircase."

I have been talking about writing this book since my son was in elementary school. At the time of this writing, he is a junior in college. Recently, my husband asked me what's going on with that dream book. My initial reaction was why is he asking, but then I realized that the only thing he was doing was holding me accountable to my own words. Why did it take me so long? I would say to myself "who wants to hear what I have to say?" "I'm not an expert." That might have been enough to keep me on the couch for that moment, but finally, I decided to claim what already belonged to me: my dream. I started acting like the person to whom God had entrusted a gift. I started accepting the call on my life and the responsibility that comes with the gift.

You have a decision to make. Do you want to take that dream

out of your head and actual take steps toward achieving it? You have a choice: it can stay a dream or you can make it happen. If you choose not to act you have in fact made a decision.

I have become reacquainted with my dream and writing this book is one of my action steps.

## LAYAWAY TAKEAWAY:

**When God gives you a dream at some point he will stir up the desire to do it. When that happens you are forced to either move or stand still, and I choose to move.**

You can always come up with reasons to justify inaction, but one of the chief reasons for inactivity is fear.

> *"Fear is the most common obstacle to achieving true success and happiness."*— Valorie Burton[1]

Sometimes you have to move in spite of the fear, and you can do it. Most people who have successfully taken their dreams out of layaway have had to move in spite of the fear.

Eleanor Roosevelt said, "Do something everyday that scares you." The irony is we are born fearless. We learn to fear. When children are toddlers they are at their most curious. That is why you constantly have to watch them. They have no fear; they will do anything. You're constantly saying "no-no" or stopping them as they explore their expanding world.

---

[1] *Successful Women Think Differently*, Valorie Burton, 2012

Some fear is healthy but as you grow older and wiser you have to move from fearing everything and cautiously move back toward that fearless childlike attitude.

*"Inaction breeds doubt and fear. Action breeds confidence and courage. If you want to conquer fear, do not sit at home and think about it. Go out and get busy."—Dale Carnegie*

*Fear can keep you trapped in the mundane monotony of sameness*

- Fear of a lack of finances,

- Fear of the future,

- Fear of the unknown

- Fear of change.

You might experience all of the above or one of them, but they are powerful and they have the potential to be crippling. My pastor says FEAR is False Evidence Appearing Real, but we believe it. We fall victim to it and it can cripple us.

## LAYAWAY TAKEAWAY:

**Fear can stop a dream in its tracks, but the key is not nursing the fear.**

Sometimes you have to make the first step. You must also recognize the many disguises that fear wears.

I was offered the opportunity to take part in a woman's

conference. There was no cost associated with participation. I only had to show up take a seat at the table and talk to women about my workshop Dreams with Deadlines. It was an opportunity to actually get out and talk about my passion and my purpose, but I initially said no. My justification was the conference had not contacted me soon enough to prepare. When they contacted me I still hesitated. It was not presented to me in the "perfect" way.

You can't afford to be a prisoner of perfection waiting for the perfect day, the perfect plan and the perfect moment.

Sadly, nothing gets done because perfection does not exist.

So stop waiting and start doing. I had to talk to myself, and say "Stop the nonsense, girl." It was an opportunity and I needed to move on it and I did. Why did I hesitate? Fear, but it came clothed in "perfection." I was justifying no action by putting the blame on something other that what it was—Fear. You've got to recognize it to make the moves you need to make. You might be scared to death, but you have to make that step. I have been talking about writing this book for years. I actually started moving. I asked myself the following questions.

1. What would I do if I were not afraid?

2. What's the worst thing that could happen?

3. What's the best thing that could happen?

4. What's likely to happen?

When you look at your situation and apply these four questions to it, you will find that it can be liberating. You will free yourself to at least try. You need to move forward in spite of the fear. I was challenged to face my fears and to actually take a leap of faith toward my heart's desire, but doing this was going to require a commitment to change.

> *"Everything you want is on the other side of fear."*—Mark Canfield

Remember, "you cannot get to your promised land until you leave your comfort zone." In some cases you might have to step over fear in pursuit of the dream. A friend of mine said she wanted to learn how to swim. She knew a little about swimming. She could float, but at some point she got tired of simply splashing around. Sure she probably was eligible for the Olympic medal for Shallow Water Swimming, but guess what? There is no medal for Shallow Water Swimming! She had to literally make the leap into the deep. Her dream was to swim and she had to take the steps – no matter how scary they might be – toward what she said she wanted to do. She had prepared herself to take the leap, but she had to get her mind to agree with her body, and she did.

## LAYAWAY TAKEAWAY:

**Fear will let you verbalize a dream, but it will prevent you from actualizing it.**

You don't want to spend half your life talking about what you are going to do, and spend the other half talking about why you didn't do it. Fear is a normal reaction, but faith is intentional. Faith is a decision. You have to commit to it. You have to walk by faith. Fear will keep you looking backwards and stop you from moving forward. Fear is going to come but it does not have to dwell. If you refuse to move because of fear you could be missing your blessing on the other side. Genesis 12:1 The Lord had said to Abram, "Go from your country, your people and your father's household to the land I will show you."

## LAYAWAY TAKEAWAY:

**Everything you need is not always in your living room. Sometimes you have to move. You'll say, "I've got my phone, my couch and my sweet tea. I'm good," but God has greater things for you if you are willing to move.**

Too often we make ourselves satisfied with the crumbs. We tolerate fake friends and fake relationships simply because we fear being alone. We surround ourselves with fearful people who feed our fears. They affirm our need to stay still, but are we giving up the abundant life God promised us.

> *"Fear is like a muscle: every time you believe a lie about yourself it becomes easier to believe another one."-Start*, Jon Acuff[2]

## LAYAWAY TAKEAWAY:

**Fear and faith can not co-exist. They are not roommates. You have to make a choice – you are going to either stand in fear or walk by faith.**

Recently I started walking with a group of determined women. We meet at 5:30 AM and walk for 30 minutes. The goal is to

[2] *Start: Punch Fear in the face, Escape Average and Do Work that Matters*, Jon Acuff, 2013

walk before you run, but it was never my intention to run. I told the ladies I am walking but we gradually incorporated jogging into our regime.

## LAYAWAY TAKEAWAY:

**Sometimes you have one dream but as you pursue that one thing you see it evolve into something bigger before your very eyes, but you will only experience evolution when you take the first step.**

Small steps lead to bigger ones and ultimately to the ultimate dream. There comes a time in your life when you have to make yourself a priority. No, you don't abandon everyone, but you do tell those closes to you that your dream is important to you and that now is the time for you to make it happen.

You are at the point in your journey where you are moving from intention to expectation. We all have good intentions, but sometimes those intentions simply don't happen, but we install a sense of urgency when we take it to an expectation. You only expect something to happen when you put in the work.

A few years ago I started my Dreams with Deadlines workshop. This workshop is specifically designed for women with dreams. This is an opportunity for women to take some time away from their busy lives and really examine what is their big dream. It is an opportunity to write the dream down, and explore ways of making it happen. We go through a step-by-step strategy as we address the factors that keep the dream in layaway. Since 2011, I have had the opportunity to see women leave energized as they crystallize a workable strategy. Today is the day to start making the dream a reality. You know it has been too long but it is never too late.

## DREAM STEPS

1.  **Learn to recognize fear.**

2.  **Learn to move in spite of fear.**

3.  **Faith and fear can't co-exist.**

4.  **Now is the time to make the dream real.**

# CHAPTER 2

# The Burden and Blessing of the Dream

It is interesting that as children we are encouraged to dream big. When young children say what they want to be or do when they grow up, their big dreams are often greeted with affirmation. People tend to smile and offer words of encouragement, but when an adult verbalizes a big dream often people will roll their eyes or openly mock the person, and sometimes this can cause you to stop and evaluate the merits of the dream. Remember, they did not give you the dream, and you should not let them take it from you or downsize it for you. You serve a mighty God who can do amazing things through those who make themselves available to Him.

Some people have you in a box. They have placed you in their own box of comfortable. It is the place where they feel most comfortable having you. When you attempt to leap out of the box they discourage you, but you have got to do it because that is the only way you can walk toward your dream. When you decide to move you are often faced with moving some of those well-meaning people out of your life.

## LAYAWAY TAKEAWAY:

**Your dream is big and it is going to call for you to do new things and some of those well-meaning folk in your life are not ready for this shift.**

The atmosphere is about to change and people are either going to be able to make the shift with you or they are not, but their actions have dictated yours for far too long. Get ready because in order for this to happen change is going to happen. You have got to accept that for your life to change you have to change what you are doing.

Some people are going to tell you they are "keeping it real" when they question your dream, but I have found too often when people say this, what they really are doing is "keeping it real negative", and you have got to move in spite of it. I have heard the phrase that we have friends for a reason, a season or a lifetime. The problem is when we try desperately to hold on to the seasonal friends when their time is up. Let it go.

**Change is a struggle** and we simply don't want to struggle, but we have to learn to take comfort in the fact that for you to achieve a great victory you are going to have to struggle. No one really wants to change. Most people will only do so if they are forced to do it or if they really see the true value of making the change.

We have become prisoners of comfort, and we don't really want to move away from it. There is a reason we want to dwell in the comfort zone. It's comfortable and we spend a lifetime yearning for comfort and once we find it we do not want to let it go. But if you are committed to living the abundant life you are going to have to leave it. You still have your dream but now is the time to possess it. You have been busy with life and the dream no longer occupies a central focus in your mind, but it still occupies your spirit.

## Stick to Your Dream (Don't be a Dream Thief)

You were probably in a very different place when you put your dream in the layaway, but if this is something that still makes your heart leap, you know this is the time to take a real and true step of faith. Your dream is that one thing that you know you want to make happen and for some reason you have not been unable to make it happen. Stop saying someday I am going to work on my dream. I once heard Dr. Phil say "Someday is not a day in the week."

## LAYAWAY TAKEAWAY:

**Someday is vision without an end day, and that is no vision.**

We can also make the mistake of co-opting the dream of other people in our lives. We have to be aware that a co-opted dream will not suffice for you to fulfill your purpose. Co-opting is getting caught up in the dreams of others, and losing yourself in their dream. As a wife I want my husband to be successful so I have to fight the impulse of getting consumed in his dream if it is to the detriment of my own. The same is true for mothers and their desire for their children to be successful.

There is a heartbreaking scene in the movie *Love and Basketball*, Alfre Woodard, played the role of the stay-at-home mother who was not respected by her daughter for her choice to be a stay-at-home mom. In one scene, Woodard speaks about her dream of being a caterer, but she put it on the shelf in layaway for the family. You respect her choice, but you grieve for what might have been. You don't have to choose one or the other you have to find a way to fulfill your passion in the 24-hour day we are all given.

We want the best for our children, but if we spend so much of our mental currency on them we might not have anything left for our own dream. It is fine to rejoice in the victories of our loved ones but those are not your dream. If you have a God-given dream, you owe it to Him and to yourself to fulfill it.

## LAYAWAY TAKEAWAY:

**God wants to bless you and he wants to bless others through you but you have to be positioned to receive the blessing.**

You've got to be willing to make a true commitment to the dream. A wise preacher, Bishop J.O. Patterson Sr., once explained the difference between making a commitment and making a donation. He told the story of the pig and the chicken. The farmer wanted bacon and eggs for breakfast. The chicken was excited to provide the eggs, but he wondered why the pig was less enthusiastic? The pig explained to the chicken for the farmer to have bacon he had to make a whole hearted commitment (a life sacrifice)whereas the chicken only had to make a donation.

## LAYAWAY TAKEAWAY:

**Your dream will not require a sacrifice of your life, but it must become a central focus for you to make it happen.**

You can't afford to make donations toward the dream. Sure you will get some sense of satisfaction as you see temporal glimpses of the dream, but is that really enough? Your true commitment is essential to your success.

Noted author Kenneth Blanchard, put it this way "There is a difference between interests and commitment. When you are interested in doing something, you only do it when it is convenient. When you are committed to something, you accept no excuses, only results." Are you tired of making excuses? Are you ready to rediscover the passion you once had for the dream? At one point you truly believed that this is the dream that would make the difference between living a life and really living a life, but how do you get that feeling back?

**First you need to reclaim the dream. (Own it!)**

If this is truly something that you believe you are called to do, you have to do what it takes to make it happen. We have so many excuses as to why we can't get the dream out of layaway. So many of us say we simply don't have time. There are just 24 hours in the day. If your child walked in and told you today I have made the basketball team and we practice everyday and I am going to need you to pick me up every evening at 6PM what would you do? You would change your schedule. You would call out the troops. You would call your mama, your daddy, sister, brother, friends and neighbors. If you couldn't pick him up you would find someone who could. It might require juggling your schedule, but it is important to him and to you, so you do it. Well I am asking you to make yourself a priority and take those same juggling skills and use them to work your own dream into your schedule. Never fail to use your "village."

The day is not going to get any longer, so you have to operate smarter. Sure that sounds like a well-worn cliché, but it is true. You are not a one man band. You have resources: friends and family. Don't be afraid to ask for help. These are the same people who have heard you talk the talk for years, and they are there now to help you walk the walk.

**What are you willing to do to make it happen?** What are you willing to sacrifice? There has never been a great victory without a great sacrifice. What were you meant to do? What are you here for? What is your purpose? You have got to clarify your purpose, and this is not an opportunity to simply sit back and analyze. Have you ever heard of the "paralysis of analysis"? Don't be a victim. After the analysis is over then it is time to take action. Your dream has to be taken off the shelf and examined, and you need to determine how can it be attained. You have to learn to believe again.

## LAYAWAY TAKEAWAY:

**If God has given you the dream you don't have to ask Him to sanction it. He gave it to you and if you take the step of faith He will equip you to do it.**

You don't need to go around asking others to sanction what God has already ordained. In my Dreams with Deadlines workshops women have shared some of their dreams with me: purchasing a home, starting a ministry, hosting a television show, becoming a life coach, becoming a personal trainer, learning a new language. These are just some of the things that women dream of doing but it is still just a dream. How can you make it happen?

It's not too late. Even if Your dream has been in the layaway

16

for 20 years, and you have become comfortable with living with the memory of it, but that is simply not enough.

You have got to take it down and start really living the life you were called to live. The beauty of a dream is it won't just die a natural death. You have to make the choice to kill it by ignoring it or simply being apathetic. Your dream can happen, but it is not going to be easy, but it can be accomplished. In order to do it you need a plan and it starts with prioritizing your day.

**PRIORITIZE (How Do you Start Your Day?)**

*Facing each day with the courage of a warrior, the joy of a child and the confidence that comes from knowing you serve an Amazing God!*

Do you plan your day or does it rule you? So often we let the day simply rule us. We get up and we simply get going. We don't think strategically we just think in terms of surviving the day. We are constantly rushing around, but we seemingly do not see any tangible gains from all of our frantic activities. We need to look at the things we must do in the course of the day. Some things are inescapable. If you work outside of your home you have to go to work. If you are a mother, even if you work outside of the home, you still wear more than one hat. You have to get the kids to school, get the lunches ready, take them to school, pick them up, take them to practice, make dinner and help with homework, and tomorrow you get to do it all over again. So when do you have time to really work on your dream? You simply don't have time, but I remember something a wise man once told me regarding the phrase "I don't have time."

He said that simply is not true, **the truth is that it is not**

**a priority because when something does become a priority you will find the time to do it.**

How many of you watch at least one hour of television a night, play on the computer after dinner or simply talk on the phone in the evenings. Why not take that time to pursue your passion? You might say well that's not really a lot of time, but that's simply not true. If you devote an hour a night toward your dream that's actually 7 hours a week. That adds up and that moves you closer to your dream. You have to start really looking at a plan to make the dream a reality. I once read a sign that said "A goal is a dream with a deadline." We all have dreams. We sometimes share them with our spouse, friends and relatives. We love to talk about the fascinating "what ifs", but too often the dream withers and dies at the end of the conversation. If we think about it again we tend to rationalize why we did not take the next step. We want to do something. We really mean to do it, but we don't. What we need is a plan and a deadline.

- It is time to start looking at your dream in phases, and say I will complete Phase I by this date.

- It even helps to recruit an accountability partner. Someone you know that has your back and will "hold your feet to the fire", but will also encourage you.

- Someone who is not afraid to question you when you try to give excuses. You also need to post your deadline on the calendar, your appointment book or your iPad or your iPhone a few days prior to the due date. That way you know the day is coming up, and you need to make your deadline.

What idea have you conceived, but for some reason never delivered?

## LAYAWAY TAKEAWAY:

**It is time to stop aborting your ideas. Your life is full of infinite possibilities. We all have too many good ideas that we have refused to truly bring to fruition. They are far too valuable to take to the grave.**

Now is the time to finally stop talking about it and start doing something.

- * If it's to lose weight--Check out Weight Watchers

- * If it's to write a book-Write a page

- * If it's to go back to School-Register for a class

- * If it's to spend more time with family-Stop saying yes to overtime

Lose the mask. As you seek to retrieve your dream you will find that you might have to acquire a new attitude. For so long you have made yourself feel comfortable with the dream in theory. You have comforted yourself by thinking how nice it would be if you could actually do it, but deep down inside you know that is simply not enough. In some cases you have adopted the dreams of others, but that simply is not enough.

## DREAM STEPS

1. **Get off the couch.**

2. **Recognize and face your fears.**

3. **Change your routine**

4. **Look at your dream in phases.**

5. **Find an accountability partner.**

# CHAPTER 3

# Recognizing and Eliminating the Dream Killers

One of the things I had to look at myself when I approached talking about dream killers was if I had killed anyone's dream. I was reminded of my son Alex' Great Big Dream. My son told me he wanted to audition for American idol. Being the "good" mother I told him you have a good voice, but I don't know if you are an Idol. He said ok and as I walked away I was convicted. Who am I to kill a dream? This is one of the points I share in my Dreams with Deadlines workshop. Don't let others kill your dream. If they didn't give it to you don't let them take it away. I walked back to my son apologized, and on the day of the audition I dropped him off at 6AM for him to follow his dream.

Most dream killers are not going to come at you with hammers and knives they are more subtle than that. The key is to recognize the dream killers. They are not your enemies – more often than not they are the people you love the most:

- You

- Your husband

- Your Family

- Your Friends

- Your Job

**You:** How can you kill your own dream? You can find ways to justify non action. There are things all around you that can prevent you from moving forward, but you are still the master of your own fate, your own destiny. You have to get out of your own way and accept the fact that you are equipped to do this thing. You have to release the past and embrace your Now.

## LAYAWAY TAKEAWAY:

*When God made you He put it all within you, but you can be impregnated with greatness that never comes to term because you are simply afraid to release the dream.*

When a woman is physically pregnant, there is a set time of incubation: nine months. If you release the child too early there is a problem or when you hold it too long there is a problem. There is a harvest time and you do not want to miss it. We can look at our dreams through these same lenses. Some of us have moved too soon and perhaps the results were disastrous. So what? You may have stumbled, but you have not failed. You only fail when you surrender, when you give up. You don't want to live a life of what ifs.

**Failure is never comfortable, but sometimes it is necessary. Some failures teach you what not to do and are stepping stones toward your ultimate victory.**

Don't stop. Re-start. Some of us are waiting...

- Waiting for a sign.

- Waiting for a word.

- Waiting for the perfect time.

  The perfect time is never coming. Now is the time to act. You've prayed about it. You've thought about it. You've talked about it. Now you have to do it.

  **Your Husband, Family and Friends:** It might be hard to accept that the people you love the most and that love you the most might be your greatest hindrance in taking your dream out of the layaway. Yet, there are ways that you can actually make them your allies in moving toward your goal. If you are comfortable where you are, the people around you are probably also comfortable. But know that as you pursue your dream, you are going to experience some discomfort and so are the people around you.

  **Don't expect everyone to buy into your dream, but you will have to distance yourself from people who try to kill your dream.**

  The biblical character Joseph had a big dream and he shared it with his family:

  **Genesis 37:5** *⁵ Joseph had a dream, and when he told it to his brothers, they hated him all the more.*

Why did I include this scripture reference? You need to know you are not alone. Your dream may not always be greeted with joy. In some cases it will be greeted like Joseph's. His family was really saying "how dare you have a dream this big." They feared his dream so much that they plotted to kill their own brother.

You have to own your dream. You have to be able to stand up against the professional dream killers. They believe they are doing their job when they stand against you. In some cases they believe they are saving you from yourself, but they are not. They are not allowing you to grow. They are not allowing you to bring the dream to fruition. Although their motives might be well meaning they are actually impeding your progress. You have to be like that old lady who clutches her handbag. The only way you are going to get that bag is to pry it out of her hand. She is not letting go because she owns that bag and everything in it. She claims it, and that's what you have to do – claim it!

**Stop waiting for affirmation when your dream has already been affirmed by God.**

You also have to become a little more selfish with your most valuable commodity: your time. This is the time in your life when you have to become a priority in your own life. You also have got to teach people in your life that NO means NO, and NO is a sentence. You don't have to always offer an explanation or a justification. You have to stop listening to the voices that discourage you from action. Sometimes you hear those voices that tell you that you can't or to stop trying for so long that they have become a part of you, but it is time to do a little "surgery" you've got to cut the tape and start listening to the voice that might have been dormant but it is the one that encourages you to first try and then it encourages you to keep going.

## LAYAWAY TAKEAWAY:

**This is your time but you have got to claim it and maintain it. You have to know it might not happen overnight but it will happen if you keep on moving.**

### *Who are you letting into your life?*

Sometimes we introduce stressors into our lives. There are some things and some people in your life that you have to have in your life. Your family and your job are two things that you have to deal with, but there are some things that you have introduced into your life that you have the power to put it out of your life. A friend of mine recently started volunteering for a non-profit. What she learned is the CEO was demanding and often demeaning. My friend is no shrinking violet so she has challenged him but the real question is, is this worth challenging? Why should she continue to put up with the antics of an unhinged CEO? This is a stressor that she invited into her life, and she has the right to invite this stressor out of her life. Time is something we can not afford to waste. You can't get it back so you have to use it carefully. Sometimes you are actually doing something good, but you have to ask yourself the question is it good for you? Does it move you toward your goal or away from it? Do you really have to keep doing it? If the answer is "No," move on.

**Don't get caught up carrying the bucket for someone else's dream. STOP...Your time is too precious and your mind should be used to move you into the direction of your dream.**

You have the right to invite someone into your life and you also have the right to invite them out. Exercise your rights!

## You have to **close the adoption agency**.

You have to stop adopting everyone's emergency. Example: You are working at home and you decide that in the morning you will be researching marketing ideas for the book you are writing but your husband keeps calling you asking you to do different tasks throughout the day. You might have to have some difficult conversations with your loved ones where you stress that this is something that you have got to do. You will have to develop and stick to a schedule and you will have to make your loved ones respect the schedule.

**You can not take your dream out of the layaway if you don't change your habits.**

Your children can often be the "masters of the last minute." They need something and they need it yesterday, and far too often we are jumping around trying to make it happen. They come to you and say "I need something today." You are often compelled to leave what you are doing to go and tend to someone else's fire. Stop being the firefighting superhero. Establish new rules. Example: When you pick your children up from school ask them if they need anything before you go home. Let them know that once you park the car in your garage you will not be taking it out until the next day. Hold them accountable and let them know that you mean business. You can't allow them to run to you after dinner and say, "I need a poster board can we run to the store?" Once you establish new rules you must enforce them even with your adult children. Don't be afraid to be the bad guy. A friend of mine Venessa Jones Clemons, gave me this sage piece of advice in regard to our adult children, "There comes a point when you have managed your child's life as long as you should. At that point you need to stop being a manager and become a consultant." This is going to be hard for a lot of you.

You've worn the "SuperMom cape" for so long, it is difficult to hang it up, but you have got to do it. Recently my son called me and told me about a problem with his charge account. He went into specific detail and I asked him did he want me to call customer service and resolve it for him, and he said yes, but as I said earlier he is in his third year of college. I stopped myself and said "no you need to make the call and if you have any problems call me," and I would aid him in resolving it. This was not my problem. I am not the manager. I am a consultant and if I want to fulfill my dream I have to accept my new role and I have to make sure he understands I no longer wear the cape.

**Achieving your dream is going to require your attention. The same passion you used when you wore the cape you are going to need it as you take your own dream out of the layaway.**

**You also might have to stop buying in to who your family says you are.** Families have a tendency to label family members. Sometimes these labels are established very early in life and we accept the labels as the truth. Maybe when you were young you never finished anything, but that does not have to be the yoke that you wear forever. Perhaps you were selfish as a child that does not mean that is who you are destined to be, but we continue to let family member perpetuate the past labels as if they are gospel, but they are not. The reality is your past might have been horrible or glorious. It is over. Don't miss your blessing continuing to look in your rear view mirror analyzing what is already done. You need that energy to approach what is going on now. Watch the people who say "I knew you when". You don't need people reciting past failures, and if they feel this is their duty it is your responsibility to give them a new assignment or determine if they can be a part of this journey.

**Stop living in the box that someone else built for you.**

Burst out and be who you know you are. Be your authentic self. You also have to examine the relationships you have with your friends. Most of us have shared our dreams with our friends. We do this because we want them to know what our goals are but we also unconsciously want our friends to affirm our dreams. We seek the "buy-in." We want them to tell us that's a great idea you should pursue, but what if they don't, what do we do? You don't need anyone to validate your dream. If you continue to ask people to affirm your God-given dream you are in fact questioning God's will for your life?

**If you have a God-given dream it is up to you to make it happen.**

God has given each of us a unique gift. You have a decision to make. You can leave it in layaway or you can take it out and make it happen. We are all pre-conditioned to need praise before we can move forward. Sometimes people cannot see what you see and that is alright, but you've got to move on. The key is to keep it moving. Keep going step by step. Sometimes it will feel like baby steps but it will put you one step closer to your dream. Along the way you are seeking guidance from God and don't be afraid to reach out to people who are doing what you want to do for advice. People who are secure in who they are will not be afraid to talk with you as you take your dream out of layaway. We serve a great God who can do great things but we've got to be ready to move. We want to live out our dreams and we, in fact, are asking God to increase our territory.

So many of us are familiar with the Prayer of Jabez in I Chronicles 4:10 – "Jabez cried out to the God of Israel, "Oh, that you would <u>bless me and enlarge my territory!</u> Let your hand be with me, and keep me from harm so that I will be free from pain." And God granted his request."

**God is prepared to help you make your dreams a reality and he is prepared to enlarge your territory, but you have got to get up off the couch.** Remember blessings are positional and conditional. You must follow God's plan for your life and you must be where he has placed you.

## DREAM STEPS

1.  Identify Dream Killers.

2.  Identify the Stressors in your life that can be eliminated.

3.  Close the Adoption Agency.

# CHAPTER 4

# Developing the Plan

*"Build your own dreams or someone will hire you to build theirs."—Farrah Gray*

What is your plan? Do you have it written down? Habakkuk 2:2-4 it is essential to write it down and include all the steps you will need to make along the way.

Pastor Kimberly Jones-Pothier says "remember if you have a pulse, God has a plan." Just because you have not been working the plan does not mean the plan is dead. God is waiting for you. So often we wonder why is God silent when we pray...perhaps it's because he has already told us what to do and now we need to simply do it.

**Sometimes he gives us all the steps and we only need to follow, but sometimes the plan is not revealed until we actually start the walk of faith.**

Taking that walk can be difficult, and in some cases paralyzing, but it all begins with the first step. As I have walked this journey there have been times when I have questioned the plan and wondered did I truly have that something within me that would equip me for the journey.

Sometimes we start feeling victimized and we wonder why things are not working for us.

*God never said the journey would be easy but He did promise that He would be with us on the journey.*

Over the past few years I have tried to fit into the mold. I have been the square trying to fit into the round hole, but as hard as I tried it still didn't work. I have been forced to ask on more than one occasion why isn't this working? One of my close friends recently challenged me to face my fears. She has been praying with me and for me as I continued to chase the "shiny object".

*Why are you not focusing on the plan? Answer: Because the plan challenges you to be the true you.*

Not the one that simply wants to talk about the dream. Not the one that is quick to dispense pieces of information to her friends. You are always quick with a solution to everyone's situation, but your own. Don't continue to live a life of all talk. Don't get me wrong. Talking about your dream is healthy, but just talking about it is not productive. It's time to move forward with purpose.

*People have ideas everyday and many of them are good ones. Although these ideas often become the topic of discussion, they never become the object of production.*

What do I mean? It is easy to share a good idea with friends or colleagues but the implementation is the real work and so often people are not equipped for the implementation. When something becomes the object of production you get it done. You become focused on production versus conversation.

Along the way I encourage you to talk to yourself. Yes I said it...talk to yourself. All of us experience the negative self-talk – that voice that tells you that you can't do it. That voice that tells you that you don't have the right to such a big dream. We all can get tripped up by the negative voice, but listen to that other voice that tells you that you can do it. **Learn to believe in the good.**

### How do you develop the plan?

The plan will be different for everyone, but one constant is a timeline, a calendar and a deadline. When you look at your plan you need to look at it in manageable pieces. Sometimes the enormity of the vision is simply too much to absorb in one swift bite. Writing this book is my challenge. I know I have a story to tell but I have to commit to writing it and not get caught up on how many pages will it be? It might be 50 pages or it might be 500 or some number in between. It will be whatever is necessary to share the story.

**You start to feel afraid, inadequate and ill-equipped for the dream, but you are not. If you have a God-given dream you are equipped to do it because He has put everything you need inside of you.**

You simply have to be willing to deal with all the parts of the dream in the appropriate time. So let's do the first thing first.

- Write down the dream.

- What do you want to do?

- What are you compelled to do?

- What are you willing to do to make it happen?

Example: I wanted to write this book. I talked about it for years. I talked to my husband, my relatives and my friends. I talked about it so much that I started to bore myself, but I finally reached the point where talking was not enough. It was time to do it. I wrote an outline. The outline broke down what I wanted to discuss in the book, but this same strategy can be used for any dream that you might have. Your plan has been in your head for long enough. Now is the time to write it down.

**OUTLINE:** Write down the dream.

(Example) You want to become a life coach. You feel you have the gift of helping people move toward their own personal goals. Have you ever had a discussion with a life coach? Reach out to someone doing what you want to do. Most people will talk to you. Confident people are not afraid to offer mentoring advice. Have questions prepared. Is there any training that you will need? Where should you go to get the training? How long will it take? Can you take the class online? Do some research and after you have done that then determine the next step. You might have to talk to people and this might be uncomfortable for you. Being outside the box can be scary, but you have got to make that leap to get closer to the dream. I said it before and I will say it again: You'll never do anything new from that comfy spot on your couch. So get up!

**Take a step every day. Make it part of your daily routine.**

I recently started running/walking. I have exercised most of my life, but not consistently. This time I committed to a

3-day-a-week regimen. The beauty of the group I joined is they required a 3-day commitment. As I stated earlier if you want something different you have got to do something different. You have to incorporate your dream into your daily routine. Every day you brush your teeth, comb your hair and shower. These are your non-negotiables. You don't get too tired or in too much of a rush to do them. Your dream has to become part of your routine. Encourage yourself everyday. I have a blackboard in my kitchen with the words I Am and each day we come up with a third word. "I am Strong", "I am Confident", "I am Unstoppable"...you get it.

*Make a declarative statement about who you are as you approach the day and work that day toward making that statement a reality in your life.*

You have got to start believing in the good. You are good and you can do all things through Christ Jesus who gives you strength. You are capable of doing things that no one else can do because you were uniquely made with a specific God-given purpose. Only you can fulfill your destiny and walk toward your vision. There are so many people with ideas, but they never become anything but ideas. You have the ability to make things happen but you have got to commit to the dream. You have to give yourself a timeline. So often we say we want to do something but we don't put the numbers to the plan. Habakkuk 2:2-3 ..."Write the vision, and make it plain upon tablets, that he may run that readeth it. For the vision is yet for an appointed time, but at the end it shall speak."

## DREAM STEPS

1. Write it down.

2. Commit to the dream.

3. Make the dream a part of each day.

4. Develop a timeline.

5. Follow the timeline.

# CHAPTER 5

# Giving Your Dream A Deadline

In my freshman year of college I had a history class. In college you experience your first time being an independent student. The teachers give you a syllabus and it is your responsibility to do what you need to do to pass the class. So I knew I had to read the book for the entire semester but I procrastinated. I was finally reading the book the night before the final. A funny thing happened: the lights in my house went out. As a matter of fact the lights went out in the entire neighborhood. There was no storm there was simply a blackout. So what do you do when you have a deadline that cannot be changed? You find the flashlight and you read the book. That's what I did and I ended up with a B in the class. I do not relay this incident as a story of victory, because it really is a story of urgency. I did what I had to do. I did what I was forced to do. There were no other options. It was do it or fail and since my parents were only paying for four years of college, failure was not an option. So why do I tell this story? I tell it because your deadline has got to become urgent. When it becomes urgent you will have the energy and resolve to make it happen. So now that it is urgent where do you go from there?

## You need to look at a calendar and map out your strategy.

1. What do I want to do? (This is different for everyone)

2. Look at it in phases. You need to do this so you are not overwhelmed and subsequently discouraged.

3. You need to look at everything you currently are doing and determine how you will fit the steps into your life. Sometimes you will need to eliminate some of the things you identify as time wasters.

4. Write it down and include your target dates.

5. Find an accountability partner. This is a person that wants you to succeed, but they are not intimidated by you. This is a person who you trust. Give them a copy of your completed plan and discuss what you are trying to accomplish.

6. Your Accountability Partner is going to hold you accountable for what YOU say YOU want to do.

7. Mark your calendar and start working on the first element of the plan. Give each Phase a start date and an end date, and post the timeline where you can see it daily.

8. You have got to commit to establishing a new routine. You want something different so you have to commit to doing things differently.

9. Pray everyday and then define the focus of that day. There are things in our lives that have to be done and we are the ones that have to do them. But there are

some things that can be delegated to others, and in this season you have to delegate.

10. Find a scripture that works for you as a source of inspiration. Mine is *Jeremiah 29:11-For I know the plans I have for you, declares the Lord, plans to prosper you, plans to give you hope and a future.*

Another good one is *Mark 10: 27 All things are possible with God.*

11. **BONUS:** Never give up on your Dream.

You need to know that when you commit to the dream, everything will not be perfect, but it will be alright. At times there will be dust on your furniture, there will be dirty clothes in the hamper and perhaps dirty dishes in the sink, but there are people in your life who are more than qualified to help you, but you have to recruit them and in some cases draft them into service. Sometimes you get no help because you don't ask for it.

Ladies, as I said earlier, we have got to hang up the Superwoman Cape. Superwoman is a fraud. She never existed. She was an urban legend. She was a myth. You can't do it all and stop trying. You need to really look at the 24 hours you are given and carve out that precious time and save some for you and the dream. Don't be too proud to ask for help. You will find that when the people in your orbit sense that you have committed to the dream they will be willing to go that extra mile for you. Remember the dream will not just bless you, but it will bless others through you.

JONI HUDSON-REYNOLDS

# DREAM STEPS

Follow the 11 Steps Above.

# CHAPTER 6

## How do you keep going?

We all have read those books that encourage us to get started and they seemingly work under the premise that once you get started you will not stop, but that is not reality. There are things that can force you to pause and they are valid. Some of us are dealing with aging parents that demand more of our time or small children and all the things they need. Professional challenges can also sideline the dream. We might be in a situation where we have to be the life coach for family members. A few years ago my husband faced some incredible challenges in his career. The challenges had the potential to severely change our way of life. During that time my singular focus was on him and my family. We prayed together and totally relied on God to take us through that tumultuous period. We were triumphant but during that time my dream was not on my front burner and that was as it should have been, but delayed does not mean denied. After the crisis has subsided it is time to look at the calendar again and re-work the timeline.

**It is alright to pause. That is not failure. You only fail when you give up. Don't put the dream back in layaway.**

The dream is out now and you recognize it. It can work if you continue to work it. I started writing this book a while ago and there have been stops and starts but finally I am focused on the thing that I said I wanted to do. If God gave you the plan know that he will bless the plan, but you have got to be in the position to be blessed. Remember blessings are conditional and positional. You have to be following God – that is the condition – and you have to be doing what He told you to do and in the place He put you that is the position. Too often we get out of position. Some of you will need other people to help you fulfill your dream, and you might be discouraged because you have not made that connection. That might lead to you stopping what you are doing, but don't! Stay faithful to the plan and you will make that connection but if you put that dream back in layaway you will not be victorious. Often when we get sidelined fear will rise again, but we talked earlier about fear but we need to address it again.

**Fear has a paralytic grip and any chance it gets to rise up it will and you have got to be ready to combat it.**

Know that you can do it. My pastor, Samson Doolin, said something recently that struck me: "Accomplishments are more than a matter of working harder, it is a matter of believing right." Do you really believe in the dream? If the answer is "yes" start again. Revise the plan, discuss it with your accountability partner and revise the timeline. You have to know this is your time.

You have been dormant and silent for long enough. It is time to do it.

Richard M. Devos said "The only thing that stands between a man (woman) and what he wants from life is often merely the will to try it and the faith to believe that it is possible."

Do you believe it is possible? Answer the question. If you say "yes" you are ready to start again. Joel Osteen said, "Fear and Faith have something in common, they both ask you to believe in something we cannot see." To make the dream happen you must continue to walk by faith and not by sight. Notice the Bible says we walk by faith. We don't run. If we ran we might miss the mission. This is a journey we have to walk. It is not a sprint, it is a walk, and along the way we will learn what we need to know to be victorious in our pursuit of the dream. This book started with a blank page and it absolutely terrified me. Why? Because I did not believe I had enough in me to share. But I simply took the first step and started sharing. You've taken the first step now you have to keep on stepping.

## Fear and Your "Right Calling"

What is your calling in life? Some people would answer this question by saying what they do, but is that your "right calling." Sure there are some things you do well but that does not always equate with your "right calling." Your "right calling" is that thing that is in you that is linked to the big dream that you have. You've gotten started and you are now moving toward one of your deadlines, but you wonder what will be your next step. You are asking yourself "How will I keep going? Will I make the right connections? Will I have the right resources? Will I have enough money when I need it?" Fear is going to be there ready to creep up, but you have got to know you have a call on your life. You have the "right calling" and this is something that is ordained by God. Fear wants you to question it but that is what kept the dream in layaway for so long. For years I heard the phrase fear of success and I never believed it possible, but it is. Some people will walk out their plan and be within the finish line or just around the corner from victory and simply stop. You have to know that your big dream is possible. Having the dream is a gift but making the dream real is going to take hard work so you have got to prepare yourself for the journey.

## DREAM STEPS

1. Don't give up.

2. Stay focused.

3. Claim your calling.

4. Prepare for the journey.

# CHAPTER 7

## Owning The Dream

Whose dream is it? Are you ready to take ownership of the dream? What do I mean? Are you really ready to make this a major part of your life? You've taken the dream out of layaway, you have become reacquainted with it and you are making moves toward making it happen, but do you really own it? One day while writing the book my uncle called me. He asked if I was busy and I told him no but I went on to say I was writing. He asked writing what and I told him I was working on a book. He replied who are you Plato? We had a good laugh, but later I had to re-examine the conversation and see how I was actually discounting my dream. I should have said yes, I am busy writing my book and I will call you back.

**You have got to respect your own dream.**

I used to feel pretentious when I would reference the fact that I was writing a book. I had to start owning the dream. This is what I was doing and I should not be afraid to accept it. If you have made the commitment and are really working the dream you have to own. Don't let fear keep you from accepting the calling. I remember I told a friend of mine

45

that I was a writing a book and she laughed in my face, but I did not need her affirmation in order for me to work on my dream.

**So be ready to own you dream not defend it. You don't have to defend it. Defending means you have to justify the "why" to others and you have done that for far too long.**

You are working it now and you have to accept everything that goes along with ownership. When you own something you don't easily let it get away from you. I own my handbag and I don't let anyone go into it without my permission. My husband and my children do not violate that rule. If they need to go into it they ask me and they know if I say yes it is for that time and that time only. It is my personal property. If I were walking down the street and for some reason someone tried to take it I would fight to hold on to it. I would refuse to let it go because I own it. That is how you have to look at your dream. Whatever it is you have to protect it and refuse to let others discount it, disrespect it or destroy it. It has been in layaway too long and you are now in full possession of it so you have got to own it. So when you own something you take pride in it and you are not afraid to talk about it or share your progress. You look for ways to improve things that you own. Ways to nurture it. When you buy a new home you know there will be upkeep. You don't buy it and let it fall down on you. You watch for things you might need to fix and if you can't do it you call a professional. That's what you do with your dream don't be afraid to call in a professional.

**Don't be afraid to reach out to someone that is doing it. Don't be afraid to ask for help.**

This is your dream we are talking about. It belongs to you

and only you. We all own a lot of things and sometimes we do neglect them. Sometimes when we are ready to use that thing we ignored. It is no longer workable or useable and we throw it away. It simply became the victim of neglect. You might have neglected that dream, but it is not ready to be discarded. You might have given up ownership in pursuit of something else. You might have a very successful career that has demanded all your attention, but you still have that dream. Often we put our all into gaining that visible success. When people look at you, they might be envious and wish they had what you have, but they do not know what you gave up to get what you have. They don't know the price you paid. Sometimes the dream is sacrificed in pursuit of the dollar, and often this can not be helped, but you have got to recognize that you will not look back on you life and wonder how could I have made more money? You will probably wonder what if I had...? Nothing is more pitiful than a life of what ifs? Again I encourage you to stay faithful to the dream. Along the way people might say hurtful things to you. Even the people closest to you, but you have to keep your dream front and center. For too long you have neglected it and now it is to time to put your laser focus on it. You own it. It's yours. It is time to do it.

## DREAM STEPS

1. Stop defending the dream.

2. Own it. Respect it.

3. Don't be a victim of "what if".

4. Be Strong.

# CHAPTER 8

# Living the Dream

The dream is out of layaway. Now what? You have got to incorporate the dream into your life. By now you have committed to change, but we all know that change is constant and your situation has changed since you embarked on the dream journey. So how do you keep going? How do you stay inspired? You are in a critical phase of the dream. You still have your responsibilities but you have taken the dream out of layaway, and you are making it happen.

You have positioned yourself for success. You have fully recognized that you were created to do exceptional things.

There is a song called "Ordinary People" by the late Dannibelle Hall. It talks about how God uses ordinary people. It specifically references the little boy who gave his meager meal of five loaves and two fishes to Jesus. Once this was placed in the Master's hand, it became enough food to feed 5,000 men. Prior to doing this Jesus prayed and he had the people get in the right position. He didn't say "let's eat" and let the crowd run wild he told them to sit in an orderly fashion.

**To make the dream happen you have to be in the right position.**

The key to your success is being in the right position. Sometimes positioning calls for us to do something: sing a song, go to school, move or change a job. **Often positioning calls for us to do something <u>we really don't want to do.</u>**

We might be comfortable just where we are, but God has bigger things for us, and He can't give them to us because we refuse to move. We wonder how do people achieve and receive their blessings. We look at our lives and say "who am I" or "I'm so ordinary" He can't use me, but that is the kind of person God wants to use, but you have got to make up your mind to get in the right position. You've finally got your mind right and you have become fully persuaded that you can do this. So how do you stay on track?

1. You have the dream defined-You know what you should be doing.

2. You have identified your accountability partner (AP).

3. You have discussed the dream with your AP. Your AP is reaching out to you. Your AP will also be a source of encouragement.

4. You are going to have to encourage yourself. You have got to believe you can do it. You have got to know you are worthy of the Big Dream.

5. You have to make it a priority.

6. You have to make it a daily part of your schedule.

## DREAM STEPS

Follow all the steps listed above.

# CHAPTER 9

# Working the Dream

How do you work the dream? Answer: Daily. Your life is not going to get less busy. So how are you going to make it work? The answer is going to be different for everyone, but some things are universal. You are going to have to commit to sacrifice. Sacrifice is not a popular word these days. We want what we want and we want it now. We will work for some things but if we have declared that this is the time of completion, we have to put some things to the side in pursuit of the dream. There are going to be some things you want to do and places that you want to go that are simply not going to be possible.

**You are going to have to learn that No is in fact a sentence that you are going to have to incorporate into your vocabulary, and it is alright.**

There many things that you are doing in the course of the week that you don't have to do. We fall into the rut of the familiar and if we stop and actually look at what we are doing, we will see the things in our lives that can be eliminated and need to be eliminated. Just as you are learning to say "no" you also have to learn to say "yes." Yes to the things that will move you closer to your dream. Fear is not going to stop trying to stop your progression. It will actually stand up throughout the process. As you move closer to the dream you will experience anxiety. The phrase fear of success has always seemed like a far-fetched concept. Who could be afraid of success?

But as you move close you might start feeling a case of the what ifs, and the mind will start working overtime. You have to keep in mind that this is a step-by-step process. Concentrate on the process. Don't get caught up on what will you do after the project is real. Stay focused on making it happen. Too often people will stop in the process because they feel they can't do it or for some reason they are not worthy of it. You have to visualize completion. For too long this big dream was simply in your head. It is out of your head and you are out of the box. This might be the time that you incorporate some other people into the mix. Gather a focus group of your true friends – the people who have your back and find joy in seeing you succeed. Roll out the dream to them and listen to the feedback. Ask for honesty. Keep in mind you are not seeking affirmation. This will come to pass but you want their reaction. You need to explain to the group exactly what you are asking them to do. Analyze their responses and if you see the validity in some of their responses you can make adjustments. But never forget this is your vision; don't surrender it.

We all have friends with big personalities and they have the capacity to be captain of the ship, but this is not their ship. They are merely passengers. You are running this and don't forget it. Listen to wise counsel and keep moving forward. Don't forget to celebrate the victories along the way. Yes this is hard work, and as you move forward don't be afraid to pat yourself on the back. You are finally doing what you were meant to do and this is worthy of celebration.

## DREAM STEPS

1. You will have to sacrifice.

2. Don't fear success.

3. Stay focused.

4. Visualize completion.

5. Congratulate yourself on the journey.

# CHAPTER 10

## The Big Dream

Finding my way to this place has been a journey. As I said at the beginning of the book I have been talking about writing this book for years. It is finally written and it is part of my big dream. This is my action step. My family and friends have been supportive, but I was the one who had to get off the couch and write the book. There were times when I doubted myself, and you will experience those times, too, but know that this is normal. Don't give up. Make the first step and then keep on stepping. Your big dream is possible but only if you make it possible. Stop looking back and saying I should have done this or that. If you are going to do it, you've got to focus on the future. You have to learn to silence the voices in your head that tell you to stop. This is work but it is moving you to your dream. I encourage you to celebrate milestones along the way. Remember each day is a gift and another opportunity to make your dream real. Remember everything may not be perfect, but if you wait on the perfect time, your dream will live and die in layaway. My dream was in layaway while I lived my life but there came a point when the dream has got to be let out of layaway so that it can grow and prosper. Sure you can live with the dream in the layaway, but why would you want to do that? You can have a life or you can have an abundant life. You can do what you were meant to do. You can fulfill your purpose. You have to put yourself in the position to listen.

It is interesting that when we are young we tend to postpone our dreams in pursuit of the Now. You just finished college and you might feel pressure to make some "real money". In your thirties and forties you are in pursuit of the home, 2 cars and 2.5 kids. In your fifties you are putting those kids through college, and in your sixties you are preparing to relocate to the most friendly retirement community, but what happened to the dream? The time in Now and this message is for everyone. Don't surrender to the rhythm of life. Write a new tune that includes your heart's desire. Your God-given purpose.

Now is the time to quiet the noise in your life so that along your dream journey you can hear from God.

## LAYAWAY TAKEAWAY:

**Face each day with the courage of a warrior, the joy of a child and the confidence that comes from knowing you serve an amazing God.**

## DREAM STEPS

1. Encourage yourself.

2. Focus on the future.

3. Quiet the noise.

4. Listen.

5. Enjoy the journey

# CHAPTER 11

# Be Encouraged

Having a dream is the easy part. Making it real will take work. Today, I encourage you to do the work. God put a dream within you at birth. Each of us was born pregnant with possibilities, but it is up to us to bring that dream to term.

God wants you to step out on faith and make it happen. You will be amazed at the people you will meet on the journey, but if you don't take that step the journey will never start.

God gave it to you to bless you and others through you. Don't you owe it to yourself to pursue it? Someone could be missing a blessing simply because you chose not to take the dream out of layaway. I encourage you to do it. You can do it. The first step can be the hardest, but it puts you one step closer to completion.

Every dream starts out one step at a time. It is not too late to make the dream real. Start today.

Remember, God honors commitment and completion. Do it. You can and my prayer is that you will. Stay encouraged as you pursue your own Big Dream!

*"I can believe in you, I can encourage you, I can inspire you, but I can not force you to grow…you have to want to do it."*— Joni Hudson-Reynolds

# TOP 10 NEVERS

*As you travel your personal dream journey, there are a few things you should Never say or do.*

**Never...**

1. Laugh at someone's dream.

2. Let anyone make you doubt yourself.

3. Be afraid to ask for help. It does not show weakness, it shows strength.

4. Expect everyone to buy into your vision.

5. Let fear govern your decisions.

6. Be afraid to ask why.

7. Be afraid to learn something new.

8. Be too big to admit you made a mistake.

9. Be afraid to lead.

10. Let your attitude stand in the way of your success.

BONUS: Never give up!

Printed in the United States
By Bookmasters